The *Spiritual* ABC's

of

Transformational Leadership

(Pre-K through 5th Grades)

by

Dr. Tekemia Dorsey

Illustrations by Hana Albrecht

Copyright © 2010 Dr. Tekemia Dorsey

All rights reserved. No part of this publication may be reproduced, stored in a retrieval system, or transmitted in any form or by any means, electronic, mechanical, photocopying, recording, or otherwise, without the prior written permission of the publisher.

ISBN: : 978-0-9843522-2-7

LCCN: 2010903223

$25.00

Published by:
Creative Creations Consulting Publishing Company
P. O. Box 9671-4017
Baltimore, Maryland 21237

www.cccpublishing.org

Printed in the United States of America, Canada, and the United Kingdom

Author's Biography

Dr. Tekemia Dorsey is the CEO/President of *Creative Creations Consulting, LLC.* and *Creative Creations Consulting Publishing Company, LLC.* Dr. Dorsey holds a Doctorate of Management in Organizational Leadership from the University of Phoenix. Dr. Dorsey possesses a Master's in Education and a Bachelor's Degree in Criminal Justice from the University of Maryland Eastern Shore (UMES). Dr. Dorsey developed and wrote the curriculum for the *1st Leadership Institute for Elementary and Middle School-Aged Children* in the country. Both of these programs are currently being executed in schools in the state of Maryland. Dr. Dorsey's life's focus includes developing programs for those less fortunate and helping others to achieve and maintain their life goals and objectives, such as the youth. In 2007, Dr. Dorsey coined the phrase; *True Leadership Lies in the Power of the Holy Spirit* © 2007.

Dr. Tekemia Dorsey is the author of *A Systems' Thinking Approach to Closing the Achievement Gap for ALL Students* **and** *Testimonies From The Knowledge Workers (Teachers): Recipes for Educational Success*. Both of these books were released in 2009. Dr. Dorsey is also the author of a weekly newsletter publication entitled Inside Leadership. The focus of the newsletter is a cross topic of issues and strategies focusing on parents, youth, education, and the community. She is proud to present her latest books, which are geared towards youth and young adult. *The Spiritual ABC's to Transformational Leadership (Pre-K through 5th Grades)* and *The Spiritual Guide to Transformational Leadership (6th through 12th Grades)* are set to release March 15, 2010. The books can be purchased from Dr. Dorsey at drdorsey@creativecreationsconsulting.com or at 443-413-5600. Please visit her website at www.cccpublishing.org or www.creativecreationsconsulting.com for more information.

Dedication

This book is dedicated to my Lord and Saviour; my Heavenly Father; and my best friend Jesus Christ. For without Him, I am nothing. I thank you Lord for the vision a few months back and for allowing the vision to now be a part of reality.

To my children, Brandon, Heaven, Halee, BJ, and Armani, I love each of you more than life itself and I hope that you are inspired and remain encouraged throughout your lives. I charge each of you to live your dream and the dreams given to you by God, to the fullest.

To my husband, Marvin, thank you for sharing in the excitement of this project and encouraging me along the way. I love you always.

Acknowledgements

I would like to give a hearty thanks to my illustrator, Hana Albrecht. This is Hana's second book project with me. Our first book project is entitled *The Spiritual Guide to Transformational Leadership (6th through 12th Grades)*. Hana is a student at Goucher College in Baltimore, Maryland. Hana is a wonderful and extraordinary artist that does outstanding work. Thank you, Hana for such wonderful and colorful illustrations on this project. I am honored to have worked with you and I look forward to a lasting and prosperous working relationship.

I would like to thank Community College of Baltimore County for offering online courses for adult learners. Through one of their online courses, I was able to learn how to self publish and start my publishing company, *Creative Creations Consulting Publishing Company*. Within a short few weeks, the book was formed, the illustrations to the book were completed, and my publishing company was birthed.

I would also like to give thanks to Gary Hines and Dolores McElroy that assisted (blindly) in the color enhancements and the layout of the book for print for this book as well. Your assistance has been appreciated and I truly thank you both. Thank you to my book reviewers that came through when needed, even though your schedules were just as busy as or busier than mines. Thanks to Dawn F., Yelva B., and Lisa P. Your mercy and grace will forever be endured.

To my hairstylists, Erika K. Harrison of Diva's & Company, thank you for making sure my hair remains healthy and strong each week. You're the best stylist in the world. To Shemeika Johnson of smjmakeovers.com for providing flawless, natural tone colors for my photo shoot. You continue to do wonderful things and you bigger break is yet to come. Keep the FAITH! Thanks to Nathaniel Isaac of uniquephoto.com for doing a wonderful job on my photos for the book and marketing purposes. God has a way of bringing everyone together for the good of HIS work. Thanks everyone from the bottom of my heart.

I give God all the praise, glory, and honor.

For without Him, I remain nothing.

x

Description of Book

This book is designed to be a teaching tool for youth; to educate and to teach them the characteristics and traits of transformational leaders because today's youth are tomorrow's leaders. Transformational leaders are leaders that work in the best interest of others, such as Jesus Christ and the Holy Spirit. There are several aspects of the book that will assist a youth to be empowered, encouraged, and enlightened. Issues such as teen pregnancy, bullying, peer pressure, gang violence, and obesity are just a few of the issues that plague youth in education. Youth need a teaching tool to help them transform themselves and the environment(s) around them. We must continue to prepare youth to take their places in society. This book is designed to assist with this goal.

The storyline of this book is geared towards helping *Preschoolers through 5th* graders gain the familiarity and ability to identify characteristics of leaders that they will one day exhibit within themselves. The biblical verses presented in the book are from the New International Version of the Bible but highlights only a variation of the passages from the scriptures.

The 1st aspect includes *Character Education* words used to describe the attributes and characteristics of transformational leaders. The 2nd aspect includes *bright, vibrant,* and *wonderful* illustrations that assist in bringing to life the other aspects of the book. The 3rd aspect includes *unique memory verses* that compliment the other aspects of the book. The 4th aspect remains the *author's biblical connections* that stems from over 20+ years of experience, knowledge and education. The 5th aspect highlights *biblical characters* that reinforce the attributes and characteristics of transformational leaders from a biblical sense. The 6th aspect helps the youth to know the books of the bible from the Old Testament and New Testament that coordinate with the letters of the alphabet.

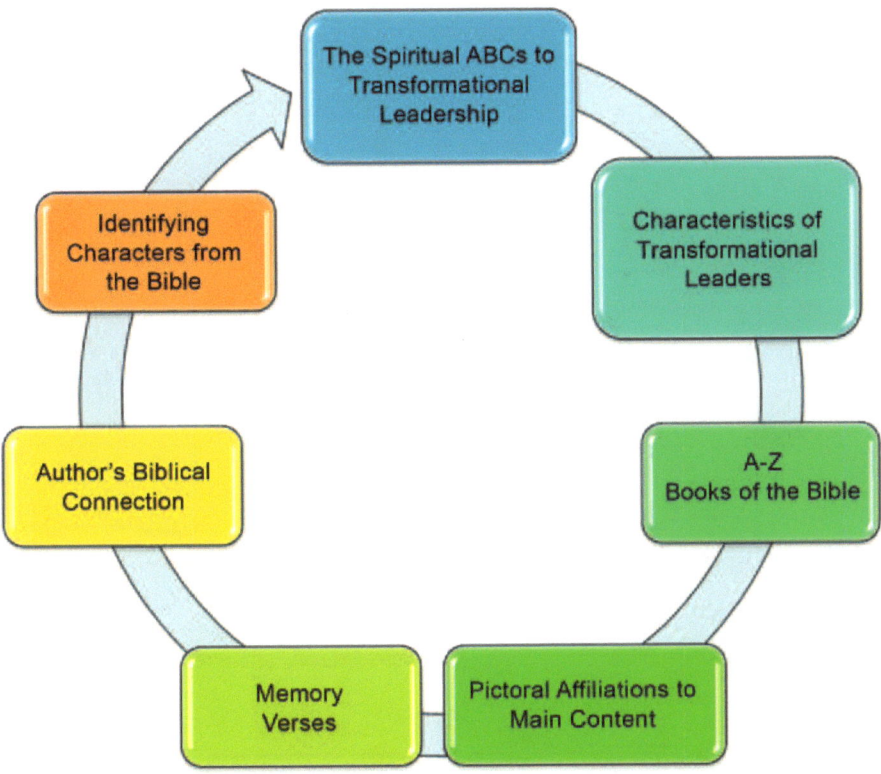

This book is the 1st book produced from part of the concepts taught in *The Leadership Institute for Elementary and Middle-School Aged Youth Programs.* *The Leadership Institute for Elementary School-Aged Youth Programs* were originally developed and piloted in 2007 (by the author) for elementary school-aged youth and was later expanded to include middle school students in 2008. I believe that leadership training and education can be taught on any level. The programs are entering their 4th year of execution in a Baltimore County Private/Christian School. Students that take part in *The Leadership Institute for Elementary and Middle-School Aged Youth Programs* are given leadership words each lesson to reflect on and to learn from. The ABC's to Leadership presented throughout this book represent key words that describe theactions and behaviors of past, present, and future leaders and are original to the Leaderships' curriculum and program. While the key word list is not inclusive, it is a good beginning to understanding the traits of transformational leaders needed for the youth of our country.

True Leadership Lies in the POWER of the Holy Spirit!

© 2007 by Dr. Tekemia Dorsey

Foreword

Children are moldable. I'll never forget the day one of my mentors said this to me. I've thought about this simple statement often and have discovered that within these few words lie power and promise. For a brief time, this mentor and I taught Sunday school together. Each week, with the help of the Holy Spirit, the eyes of children were opened to truth. Children sat attentively as the word of God molded and shaped them for kingdom living. For 52 Sundays a year, through consistency and prayer, we planted precept upon precept into their hearts and minds. Today, we praise God for the harvest of young people who are advancing the Kingdom.

I believed then, and still believe today, that the word of God is useful for teaching. I've discovered that the best lessons are the ones that can be applied to everyday living. In *The Spiritual ABC's of Transformational Leadership*, Dr. Dorsey has taken something as familiar as the ABC's and created a model for how children can become leaders, who are obedient to Christ, children who can transform the world through Christian leadership. As children read this book, they'll make connections between the word of God and Bible heroes. They will also discover that godly character is not just an attribute for adults but for them too.

I am witnessing, first-hand, the fruit that is blooming in the lives of children that have been exposed to *The Spiritual ABC's of Transformational Leadership*. This is surely the Lord's doing and it is marvelous in my sight!

Min. Yelva Burley
Servant to Children & Youth
United Baptist Church, Baltimore, MD

Preface

To the reader, our youth, and your children are the center of the world and for that, we, in my opinion are obligated to assist in making a difference in their lives in every possible way. They are the creatures on Earth, closest to God's heart and are as pure as the fallen snow. We remain responsible for molding and shaping the youth to be in God's kingdom what they are destined to be. The children today are quite different than the children of yesterday. In the former days, the parents, grandparents, neighbors, uncles and aunts all played a part in the rearing of a child. It took the village to raise the child and the hands of many were in actuality that village. For today's youth, this view is not shared or believed among the majority. This remains one of my greatest concerns.

Through the concerns I share amongst many parents, educators, leaders, and those in ministry, this book serves as another tool to teach and educate our youth. The contents of the book can help youth to understand characteristics of leaders and also learn memory verses that will stay with them forever. Not every child has an entourage of adults surrounding them to share, witness, and provide the basics and foundation of life. While the contents of this book is in no where a means to an end, it remains another step in the right direction. I hope that youth and their parents remain blessed with the teachings and equations of the story.

This book is designed for parents, ministries, leaders, educators, school systems, and anyone that come in contact with our youth. The targeted audience for this book is Preschoolers through 5th grades. Parents can begin teaching and reading to their child at the onset of conception; this is true as I am a witness of the successful outcome. I hope this book is a blessing to the reader and the one reading it.

Memory Verse
All Things Are Possible Through Christ Who Strengthens Me.
(Matthew 19:26)

Transformational leaders are those that display positive **attitudes.** Examples of transformational leaders with positive **attitudes** are your mommies and daddies.

Biblical Character
In the book of Genesis, **Adam** had a positive **attitude** towards God!

Books of the Bible
The book of **AMOS** is in the Old Testament; the book of **ACTS** is in the New Testament.

Memory Verse
***Believeth** in the Lord Jesus Christ, and thou shalt **be** saved.*
(Acts 16:31)

We must learn to be **brave** in the midst of negativity and fear, for GOD is always with us. Transformational leaders are those that have **brave** hearts.

Biblical Character
Bathsheba was the beloved wife of King David and the mother of Solomon.

Books of the Bible
There are no **books** in the Old Testament or New Testament that **begin** with the letter **B.** However, the **Bible** itself begins with the letter **B.**

Books of the Bible
The book of *Colossians* is in the New Testament.

Biblical Character
Cyrus is a king, found in the book of Ezra who was *courageous* and that *cared* for others.

6

Memory Verse
__Children__ obey your parents in the Lord for this is right.
(Ephesians 6:1)

We must learn to have the **courage** to stand up for ourselves and to **care** for others. Transformational leaders are those that have **courage** and **care** for the best interest of others. An example of a transformational leader is Jesus the **Christ.**

Memory Verse
***Depart** from evil and **do** good.*
(Psalm 34:14)

Transformational leaders are individuals that are **determined, dedicated** and **devoted** to things they believe in. An example of a transformational leader that is **determined, dedicated,** and **devoted** are grandparents to their families.

Biblical Character
David was a character in the bible that was *determined, dedicated,* and *devoted* to God's work and HIS kingdom.

Books of the Bible
Deuteronomy is one of the books in the Old Testament and *Daniel* is the other book in the Old Testament that begins with the letter **D.**

> **Memory Verse**
> ***Everything*** that has breathe praise the Lord.
> (Psalm: 150:6)

Transformational leaders are poised, *elegant* persons that always work in the best interest of others. Mary Magdalene was a poised, *elegant* woman that worked in the best interest of Jesus Christ.

Biblical Character

Queen *Esther* was a poised, *elegant* lady that work in the best interest of her people, the Jews.

Books of the Bible

There are five books that begin with the letter *E* in the Old Testament, which are *Ezra, Exodus, Esther, Ezekiel,* and *Ecclesiastes.* One book that begins with the letter *E* is in the New Testament, which is *Ephesians,*

Memory Verse

*This, then is how you should pray:
Our **Father** who art in Heaven,
hallowed by thy name.*
(Matthew 6:9)

Books of the Bible
There are no books in the bible that begin with the letter **F.**

Biblical Connection
We learn about *Famine* in the book of Genesis and we learn about *Feasting* in the book of Leviticus.

Transformational leaders are *fearless* of the world, but *fearful* of the Lord!

Memory Verse
*Beloved, let us love one another,
For love is of **God**; and everyone who
Loves is born of **God** and knows **God.**
(1 John 4:7)*

Managers are *good* but leaders are *great.* It is better to lead someone than to manage them. Teachers are *good* examples of those people that are *great* leaders that transform the lives of others.

Biblical Character
Goliath was the character in the bible that David defeated.

Books of the Bible
Genesis is in the Old Testament and *Galatians* is in the New Testament.

Transformational leaders are those lead by the *Holy* Spirit, while others are lead by the world. Examples of transformational leaders are pastors, deacons, and others just like you, such as President Barack Obama.

Memory Verse
The Lord said to my Lord,
*Sit at My right **hand**,*
Till I make Your enemies Your footstool.
(Matthew 22:44)

Books of the Bible

The books of the bible that start with the letter **H** are found in the Old Testament. The names of the books are *Hosea, Habakkuk,* and *Haggai.* There is one book from the New Testament and that is *Hebrews*.

Biblical Character

Haman is the character from the book of Esther that wanted to do harm to the Jews but was stopped by Queen Esther.

Books of the Bible
Isaiah is a book in the Old Testament that begins with the letter *I*.

Author's Bibical Connection
I live to serve the Lord in all things that I do and be.
Dr. Tekemia Dorsey

Transformational leaders are given wisdom and knowledge through the power of the Holy Spirit, which helps them to make *intelligent* choices in life.

Biblical Character
Izban led *Israel* after *Jephthah*. *Izban* led for seven years.

Memory Verse
Judges 13:8 says O' Lord, I beg you let the man of God (an angel) return once again.

Transformational leaders are those with *Jesus* Christ-like characteristics such as having a positive attitude, being filled with the Holy Spirit, and being fearful of thy Heavenly Father.

Biblical Character
Job was a faithful servant of Christ who believed, but was challenged at times throughout his life.

Books of the Bible
Joshua, Judges, Jonah, Job and *Jeremiah* are books in the Old Testament that start with the letter *J;* while *James, Jude* and *John* are books in the New Testament that begin with the letter *J.*

Books of the Bible
There are no books of the bible beginning with the letter **K.**

Biblical Character
King Kislev could be found in Nehemiah &
King Kadmiel can be found in
the book of Ezra.

Memory Verse
*Forgive them Lord as no one is upright and They do not **know** the way of the Lord.*
(Jeremiah 5:4)

Transformational leaders can be viewed as **Kings** because of their poise, admiration, and humbled spirits; however, transformational leaders view themselves as servants of the **kingdom** who were put here to serve others with a happy heart.

Biblical Character

*Immer is a **likable** person and servant of the **Lord** that can be found in the book of Ezra!*

Memory Verse #1
*Oh, **Lord,** do not your eyes **look** for truth.*
(Jeremiah 5:3).

Memory Verse #2
Should you not fear me declares the **Lord.**
(Jeremiah 5:22)

Books of the Bible
Lamentations and **Leviticus** are books from the Old Testament that begin with the letter **L** and **Luke** is another book from the bible but found in the New Testament that begin with the letter **L.**

Transformational **leaders** have **likeable** and **lovable** spirits that allow them to **look** out for the best interest of others. Brothers and sisters have **likeable** and **lovable** spirits that **look** out for others.

Memory Verse
*He said to me, "You are **my** servant, Israel, in whom I will display **my** splendor.*
(Isaiah 49:3)

Biblical Character
Mordecai is the uncle of Esther who fought for the rights of Jews and can be found in the book of Esther.

Transformational leaders tend to take on **monumental** tasks that they need help with such as Noah and **Moses** in the bible. **Moses** and Noah were both given enormous tasks to complete but needed help and guidance from the Lord.

Books of the Bible
The books of the bible that begin with the letter **M** are **Micah** and **Malachi** from the Old Testament and **Matthew** and **Mark** from the New Testament.

Memory Verse #1

*Let him who walk in the dark,
who has no light,
trust in the* **name** *of the Lord
and rely on his God.*
(Jeremiah 50:10).

Books of the Bible

Numbers, Nahum, and **Nehemiah** are books of the bible from the Old Testament that begin with the letter **N**. There are no books of the bible in the New Testament that begin with the letter **N.**

Biblical Character

The book of Daniel talks about King *Nebuchadnezzar's* troubled dreams during his 2nd reign as King.

Transformational leaders are *nice* to others and *not* mean.
Transformational leaders are *not naughty* and disobedient people.
Daniel, from the book of Daniel was a nice person to
King *Nebuchadnezzar,* despite how the king treated him.

Transformational leaders are *ordinary,* yet exceptional people just like you and me. President Barack *Obama* is an *ordinary* person that helps to transform the lives of *others* in the United States and around the world.

Books of the Bible
Obadiah, the book from the *Old* Testament begins with *O.*

Biblical Character
King **Og** was defeated by Edrei, who reigned in Ashtaroth. This can be found in the book of Deuteronomy.

Memory Verse
*Therefore, as we have **opportunity,** let us do good to all people, especially to those who belong to the family of believers.*
(Galatians 6: 9-11)

Transformational leaders work with *people* from all types of backgrounds such as African Americans (Black), Caucasians (White), Japanese & Chinese (Asian), Latino, Hispanic, and Native Americans. Queen Esther worked with men and women from all over the kingdom. Your parents work with *people* from various backgrounds as well. Working with *people* that are different from us, helps to make us grow as a *person.*

Books of the Bible
Psalms and *Proverbs* begin with the letter *P* and can be found in the Old Testament. *Philippians* and *Philemon* are books of the bible that are located in the New Testament that also begin with the letter *P.*

Memory Verse #1

And said, "Naked I came from my mother's womb, and naked I will depart. The Lord gave and the Lord has taken away; may the name of the Lord be **praised.**
(Job 1:21)

Biblical Character

Peter was one of 12 disciples who denied Jesus three times.

Memory Verse #2

Should not your **piety** be your confidence and your blameless ways your hope.
(Job 4:6)

Author's Bibical Connection
Quiet is the man that hears nothing.
　　　Dr. Tekemia Dorsey

Transformational leaders are often *quiet* individuals that are not *quick* to make decisions. Transformational leaders are individuals that usually think before speaking, acting and doing so is a *quintessential* (the most perfect embodiment of something) characteristic of them.

Books of the Bible
There are no books in the bible in the Old Testament or New Testament that begins with the letter **Q.**

Bibical Character
Quail is a character in the bible that can be found in the book of Exodus.

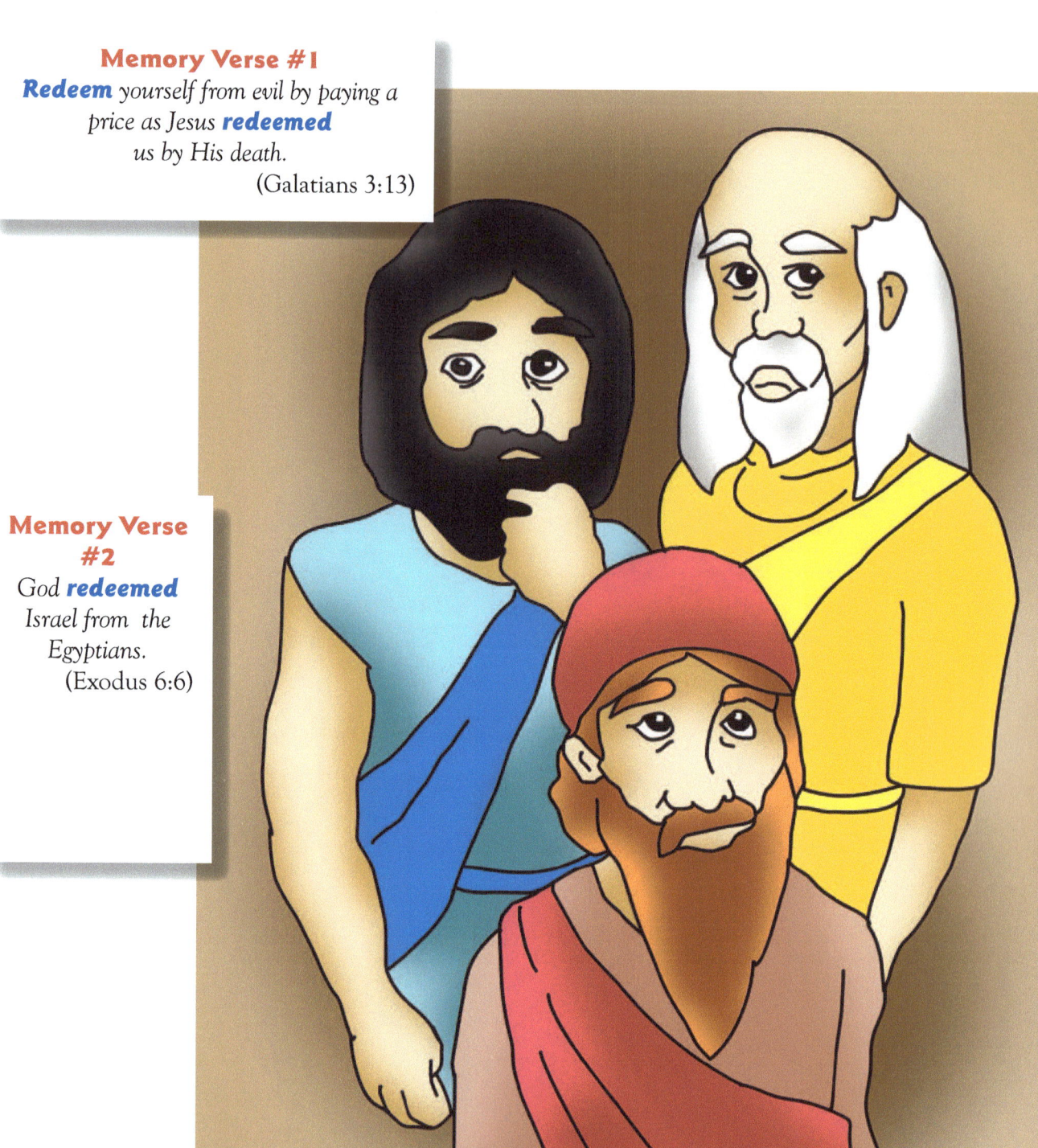

Memory Verse #1
Redeem yourself from evil by paying a price as Jesus *redeemed* us by His death.
(Galatians 3:13)

Memory Verse #2
God *redeemed* Israel from the Egyptians.
(Exodus 6:6)

Biblical Characters
Ramah, Rezin, and *Reaiah* are characters of the bible whose names begin with the letter **R** and can be found in the book of Exodus.

Books of the Bible
Ruth is a book in the Old Testament of the bible and *Romans* and *Revelation* are books of the bible found in the New Testament of the bible.

Transformational leaders are *righteous* in their efforts to do God's will in their life and in the lives of others. Being *righteous requires* a person to submit themselves humbly to God (mind, body, and spirit) and no one else.
A good example of a *righteous* person is the Pope.

Biblical Character
Samuel, Saul, and ***Solomon*** are characters
whose names begin with the letter ***S*** and can be found in 2ⁿᵈ Chronicles.
Each of these characters were ***special*** in the eyes of Jesus Christ.

Author's Bibical Connection
The ***soul*** is the ***spiritual*** part of a person that does not die.
Dr. Tekemia Dorsey

Books of the Bible
Songs of Solomon is the only book in the Old Testament that begins with the letter ***S***. There are no books in the New Testament that begin with the letter ***S***.

Memory Verse #2

Surely, He will save you from the fowler's snare and from the deadly pestilence, He will cover you with his feathers and under His wings you will find refuge; His faithfulness will be your shield and rampart.

(Psalm 91: 3 & 4)

Transformational leaders are *smart, sophisticated*, and blessed persons who do not mind sharing God's testimonies with others. Transformational leaders are not afraid to *shout* God's holy name with others.

Author's Bibical Connection
True Leadership Lies in the **POWER** of the Holy Spirit.
Dr. Tekemia Dorsey

Transformational leaders stay *true* to who *they* are and continue to evaluate *themselves* as frequent and often as possible.

Books of the Bible

The book of the bible that begin with the letter *T* is *Titus* found in The New *Testament*. There are no books of the bible that begin with the letter *T* in the Old *Testament.*

Biblical Character

In the book of Philemon, Paul's associate *Tychicus* escorted Onesimus and delivered the letter to Philemon.

Books of the Bible
There are no books of the Bible that begin with the letter **U.**

Biblical Character
Uzziel is a character in the bible and can be found in 2 Chronicles.

Memory Verse #1
*For HE has founded it **upon** the seas,
and established it **upon** the waters.*
(Psalm 24: 2)

Memory Verse #2
*Give **unto** the Lord, O you mighty ones,
Give **unto** the Lord glory and strength.
Give **unto** the Lord the glory due His name;
Worship the Lord in the beauty of His holiness.*
(Psalm 29: 1 & 2)

Each transformational leader has been created *unique* in his/her own way to complete God's will for their lives; just like you and me!

Transformational leaders are *vocal* in their efforts. Transformational leaders use their *voices* for the good of GOD's kingdom and for what is right for others in the world.

Author's Bibical Connection
Noah listened to the *voice* of God and built an Ark that was used as the *vessel* to preserve life on earth for God's creatures.
Dr. Tekemia Dorsey

Books of the Bible
There are no books of the Bible that begins with the letter **V**.

Author's Bibical Connection
When we keep God first in our lives, we can claim **VICTORY** in everything we do!
Dr. Tekemia Dorsey

Author's Bibical Connection

God finds favor in man by providing him a *wife* as his help mate.
Dr. Tekemia Dorsey

God is mighty and *worthy* of our praise and transformational leaders that *work with*, for, and alongside each of you do not mind giving God all the praise. Examples of these types of transformational leaders are sons, daughters, brothers, sisters, and cousins.

Books of the Bible
There are no books in the Bible that begin with the letter **W**.

Memory Verse
Wisdom, *like an inheritance, is a good thing and benefits those that see the sun.*
(Ecclesiastes 7: 11)

Biblical Character
Xerxes is a character in the bible that can be found in the Book of Ezra.

Author's Bibical Connection
X marks the spot in the bible when, where (finish the sentence with your favorite saying………..)
Dr. Tekemia Dorsey

Books of the Bible
There are no books in the Bible
that begin with the letter **x.**

Transformational leaders often times wear **x**-ray glasses that allow them to look beyond the transgressions of others; just like God does each one of his children.

The Letter **Y's** Special Prayer

Dear God:

*Thank **You** for loving me.*

*Thank **You** for this day*

    and the beautiful world I live in.

*Thank **You** for family and friends*

    to play and share with.

*Thank **You** for my home—*

    for clothes and food and a safe place to be.

*Thank **You** for my church*

    and for those who are teaching me.

*Dear God, help me to do what **You** want me to do.*

Forgive me when I do wrong things—

    when I hurt myself and those around me.

*Forgive me when I hurt **You.***

Make me want to be the very best that I can be.

In Jesus name, I pray, AMEN!

    @ 1984 by Thomas Nelson, Inc. Precious Moments Bible

Books of the Bible
There are no books in the Bible that begins with the letter **Y.**

Transformational leaders are God's gift to the Earth. **You** are a transformational leader. **You** are a marvelous leader sent by God to do wonderful and wondrous things while here on Earth for His kingdom. Say, **Yes,** I am because **Yes, you** are.

Transformational leaders are *zealous* in their efforts to get things done for God's kingdom.

Books of the Bible
The books in the bible that begin with **Z** are **Zephaniah** and **Zechariah** can both be found in the Old Testament. There are no books in the New Testament that begin with the letter **Z.**

Memory Verse
*Great is the LORD in Zion;
he is exalted over the nations.*
(Psalm 99:2)

Biblical Connection
Zion is a city in the bible that is redeemed by
justice and her penitents with righteousness.
(Isaiah 1:27)

Special Thanks!

I give thanks to you, the reader for taking time out to purchase and read this book. May the content and illustrations be a blessing to you and the family.

I give thanks to the parents, educators, and others for purchasing this book for their youth. May the teachings and associations in the book enhance their learning and love for the Lord and what He has in store for them in their lives.

I would like to give thanks, praise, and a hearty expression of gratitude to my heavenly Father, confidante, Prince of Peace, and bright light at the end of my day; Jesus Christ. This project has made it to completion all through Your guidance, grace, vision, and creation. Thank you so much! I remain humbled!

Author's Final Comments

From the knowledge obtained during the writing of this book, accompanied by in-depth semi-structured interviews with the knowledge learned from workers who guide and lead the students daily, teachers, I have created two leadership models aimed at teaching leadership training and education on the elementary school level and added during the 2008-2009 school year, leadership training and education on the middle school level as well. I developed the curriculum and I am now executing the 1st Leadership Institute for Elementary School-Aged Youth in the country, to date. The first leadership training model, specific populations are Christian and private schools **(see Figure 1)**. The second leadership model, specific population is the public school system **(see Figure 2)**.

The difference between the two models remains one component; categorically, which is life teachings. Life teachings from a spiritual perspective versus a secular perspective remain the difference in the two models. One of the main components missing from the public school system (from my perspective, understanding, and life experiences), even if one does not truly believe, is God and spiritual connections and relevance to the world around us; (spiritual teachings and reinforcement). Both leadership models are presented next, immediately follow by a description.

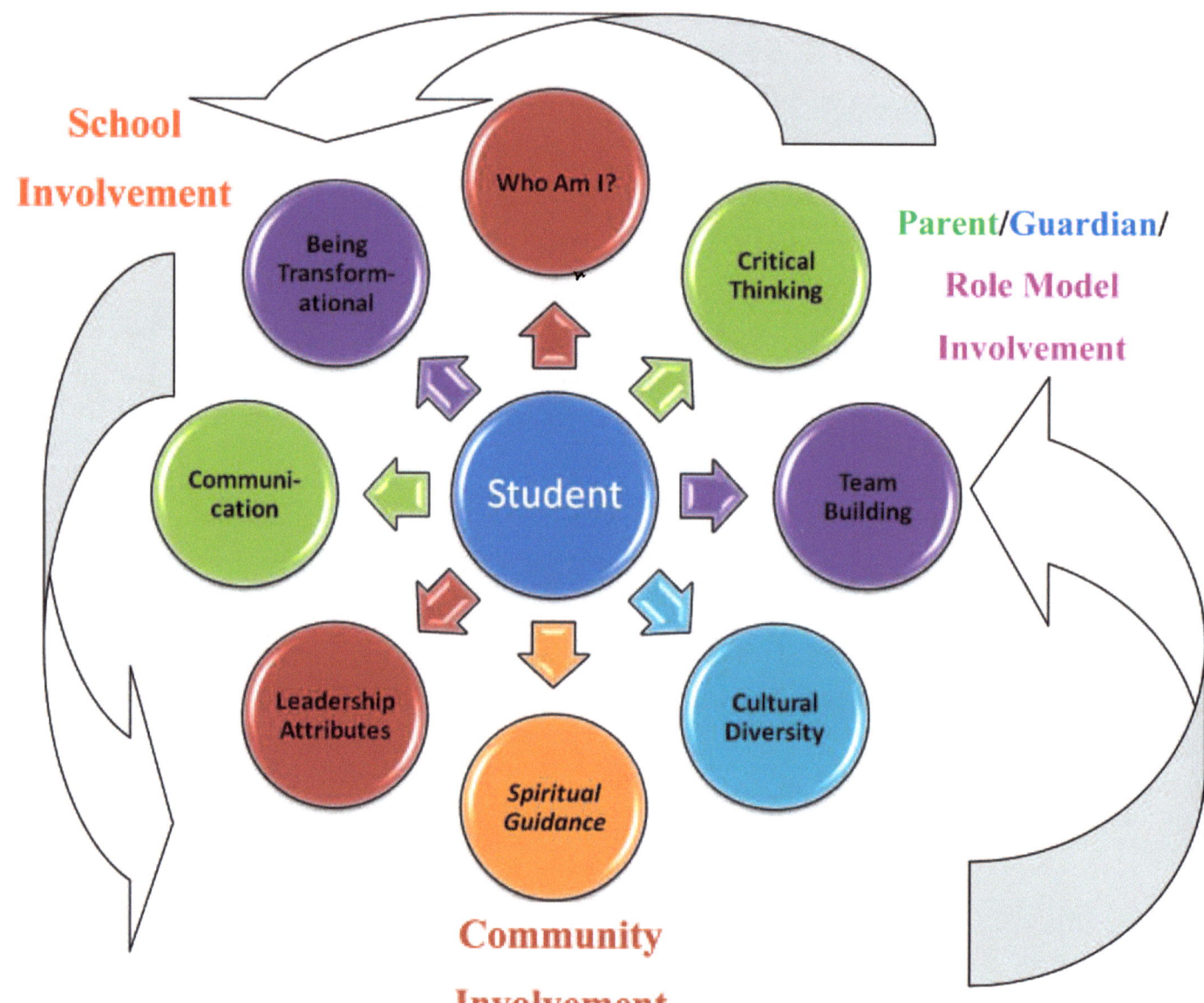

Figure 1 *(Model #1)*

Dorsey's Spiritual Leadership Training and Education Model for *The Public School System*

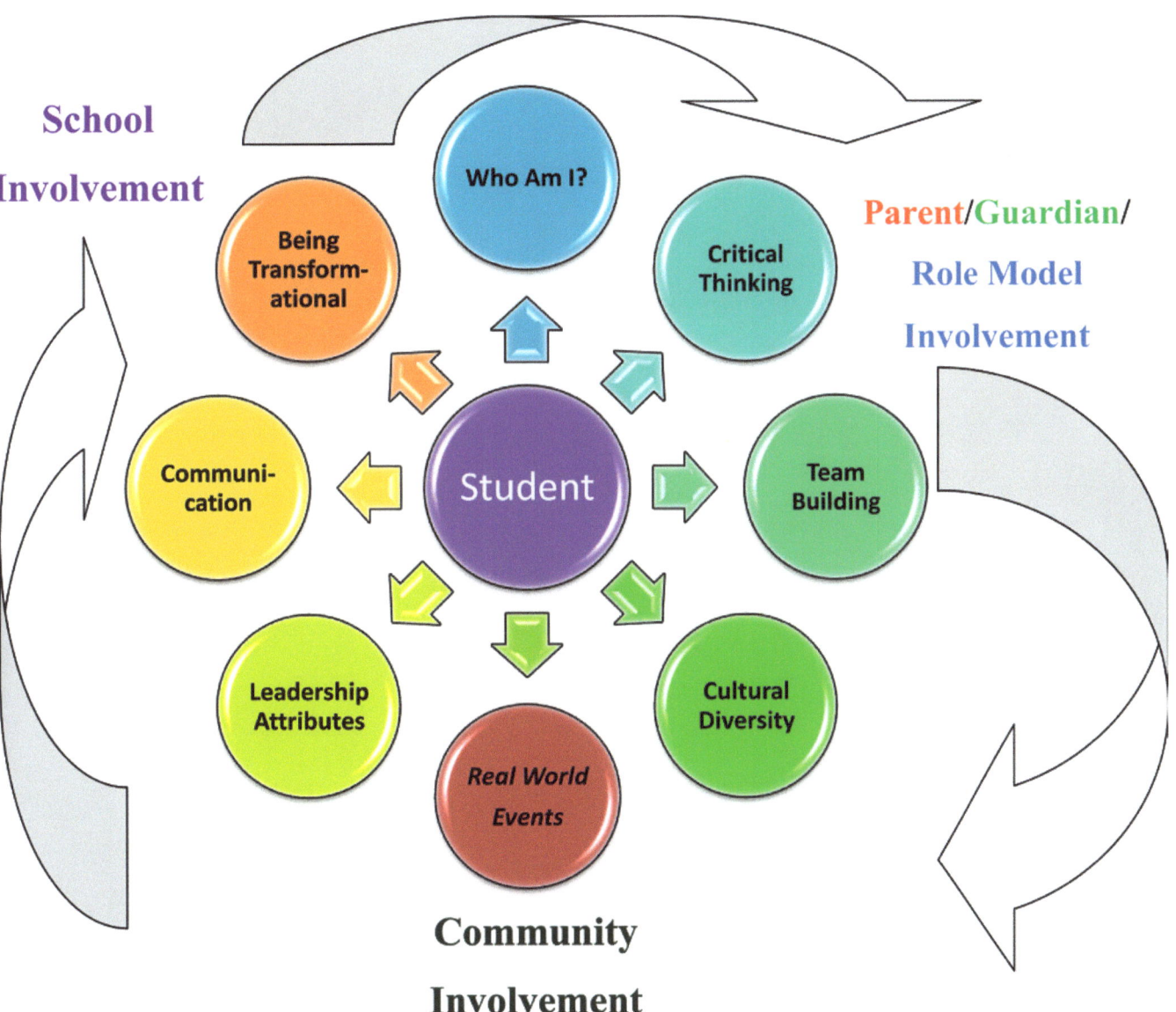

Figure 2 *(Model #2)*

Description of Dorsey's Spiritual and Secular Leadership Training and Education Models

There are three levels to each model. On the first level, the center is represented by the student. The student is the core of what matters for the next generation, in today's society, and for the models created. Surrounding the student (on the 2nd level), are eight core components to success in life. The concepts of *Who Am I, Critical Thinking, Team Building, Cultural Diversity, a Life Skills Concept, Leadership Attributes, Communication and Being Transformational* are eight attributes and skills needed for students to transition successfully into tomorrow's future leaders. The life skills concept in each model varies from *Spiritual Guidance* in the first model to *Real World Events* in the latter model. In order for the students to be productive in life and within themselves, proper guidance is needed from parents/guardians/role models, the community, and the school system, collectively, not individually. This layer represents the 3rd and outer level of the models.

Leadership model #1 was executed in a Baltimore Private Christian school through a pilot program during the 2007-2008 school year. The leadership program and pilot program were huge successes during the 2007-2008 school year. The leadership program has now been expanded to other schools in Baltimore, Maryland. From the pilot program, I coined the phrase *True Leadership Lies in the **Power** of the Holy Spirit*. Instead of the training and leadership experience being one-sided, from teacher to student, I learned from my students' tremendous knowledge and *priceless* experiences. The *Holy Spirit* remains evident in each and every lesson and throughout the execution of the program, then and now.

The findings from the in-depth, semi-structured interviews previously conducted with teachers/administrators will be published later this year and the outcome of teaching the leadership training and education program to elementary school-aged and middle school-aged youth will be released early 2010. To find out more about *The Leadership Institute for Elementary School-Aged Youth* and *The Leadership Institute for Middle School-Aged Youth* or the curriculum, please contact me at drdorsey@creativecreationsconsulting.com. It remains my hope and prayer that this program will expand nationwide and possibly internationally [overtime], so that our youth will be better equipped to lead our nation in the days to come.

www.ingramcontent.com/pod-product-compliance
Lightning Source LLC
Chambersburg PA
CBHW042025150426
43198CB00002B/67